CONTENTS

FOREWORD

The recording *The Faces of Love* came into being at the suggestion of my dear friend and colleague Frederica von Stade. We got to know each other in 1994, when I was working in the public relations office at the San Francisco Opera and writing music in whatever spare time I could find. I gave her a gift of some folk song arrangements; ever since, she has proved an extraordinary source of encouragement and inspiration. We have now collaborated in the creation of three song cycles, orchestral songs, and choral works, and she will create a major role in my upcoming opera. During one of our projects, I asked if she'd try her hand at writing lyrics. The results display yet another side to this amazing woman's creativity. To date, I have set eight of her poems, five of which are featured on the recording.

When Frederica and I discussed the possibility of a recording, she insisted that it should include all the wonderful singers who were, by then, championing my work. I had met and befriended a number of these artists through my P.R. job at the opera, and they had all offered to participate in such a project whenever the time came. They were all true to their word.

What an amazing time it is for American art song! After years of being either ignored or squeezed into recitals as novelty items or encores, songs by American composers are now celebrated and featured in concerts and recordings throughout the world. How thrilling to sit in a concert hall and hear American performers singing songs in their own language, and to feel the audience's immediate understanding and connection with the text and music. There is a tremendously rich legacy of art song in this country, and I feel fortunate to find myself writing songs at this time and to have some of America's great singers supporting my work.

For me, every song is a drama of its own, to be performed as seriously as a scene from a play or an opera. In each song I try to create a sense of the psychology and emotion behind the words in order to create a sense of character; but I also try to leave plenty of room for the performer to invest his or her own sense of the drama, whether tragic or comic.

In these songs, the singer encounters the full gamut of the influences I grew up with: folk music, jazz, pop, opera, rock, art song. I encourage performers to embrace these elements in the songs and not shy away from them. If it feels jazzy, well, it probably is. The texts range from classic writers like Dickinson, Lindsay, Sidney, Rilke and Millay, to an exciting generation of contemporary American poets including Philip Littell, John Hall, Gini Savage, Gavin Geoffrey Dillard, and of course the multi-talented Frederica von Stade.

No matter what else you may find in them, my songs are about love. They are about the different kinds of love we experience in our lives: romantic, sexual, desperate, maternal, paternal, fraternal; the love of a pet, the love of self, love of God, love of nature—all the different facets, the different faces of love.

—JAKE HEGGIE

Jake Heggie (left) and Brian Asawa

ABOUT THE COMPOSER

Jake Heggie was born in Florida in 1961 and grew up in Ohio and California. His principal teachers were Johana Harris (at UCLA) and Ernst Bacon (privately). Currently he serves as composer-in-residence for the San Francisco Opera, where he is working on his first opera, based on Sister Helen Prejean's *Dead Man Walking*, with the playwright Terrence McNally. He has composed over 100 songs as well as choral, orchestral and chamber music.

RECORDINGS

THE FACES OF LOVE: The Songs of Jake Heggie (26 songs)
RCA Red Seal 09026-63484-2
Kristin Clayton, Renée Fleming, Nicolle Foland, Sylvia McNair, and Carol Vaness, sopranos
Zheng Cao, Jennifer Larmore and Frederica von Stade, mezzo-sopranos
Brian Asawa, countertenor
Jake Heggie, piano
Emil Miland, cello

MY NATIVE LAND (includes five Jake Heggie songs for mezzo-soprano)
Teldec 0630-16069-2
Jennifer Larmore, mezzo-soprano
Antoine Palloc, piano

ENCOUNTERTENOR

John Hall

1. Countertenor's Conundrum

Jake Heggie

Quasi una fantasia

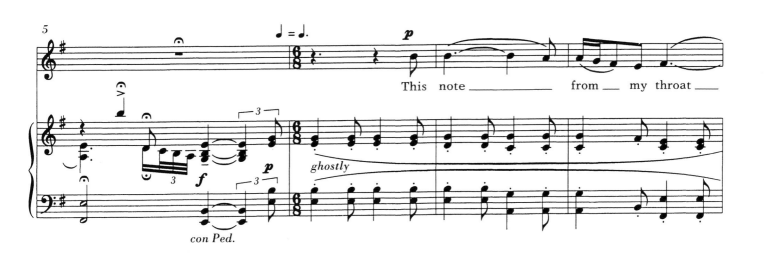

This note ____ from ____ my throat ____

ghostly

con Ped.

Allegretto grazioso

con-jures im - ag -ined mem-o-ries _____ of

al - tered males who stood up-on a stage and with _ their_ scales _____

and trills _____

Tempo I – moving ahead

pres-ent and com - plete. This note _____

this note Ah! _____ from _____ my

throat _____ you un-der-stand _____ the his - to-ry _____ that

sets my voice a - part Now

THE FACES OF LOVE
THE SONGS OF JAKE HEGGIE

BOOK 3
MEDIUM VOICE AND PIANO

AMP 8159
First Printing: April 2000

ISBN 978-0-634-01114-6

Associated Music Publishers, Inc.

DISTRIBUTED BY

HAL•LEONARD®
CORPORATION
7777 W. BLUEMOUND RD. P.O. BOX 13819 MILWAUKEE, WI 53213

2. The Trouble with Trebles in Trousers

Allegretto
(not too fast)

La la la la, _____ La _____

Ah _____

It wasn't long a - go _ that peo-ple

laughed when I would _ sing _____ They weren't un-com-f'rta-ble _ with what I _

A tempo – gracefully

teach-ers __ who spe-cial-ize in voic - es be - lieved I had some

choic - es _____ When they heard me they'd

shake their heads and won - der: How did it get so

much like a mez - zo? _____

3. A Gift to Share

for Earle Patriarco

THOUGHTS UNSPOKEN...
1. A Learning Experience Over Coffee

John Hall

Jake Heggie

poco rit.   a tempo

18
way that you will say "O. K.,   but that's not what you said _____ to-

non rit.

23
day..." _____   I love you so...   dear. You'll nev-er

28
know...   dear. That in the time we've spent to-geth-er I've but one fear,__

rit.   a tempo   rit.

32
You might dis - cov - er   Your "per - fect"

24

2. You Enter My Thoughts

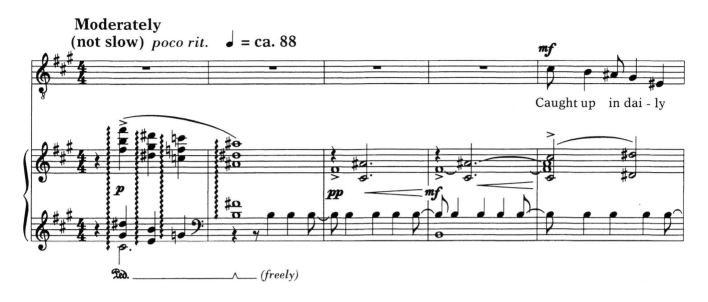

Caught up in dai - ly

life, _____ sell-ing and buy - ing work-ing and __ try-ing to __

__ cope, _____ I lose _____ hope. _____

3. To Speak of Love

say sounds wrong, sounds wrong Then mu-sic is — my on-ly hope _____ and

when you hear this song Know __ that it says I love you, says I need you. Just

un-der-stand one thing

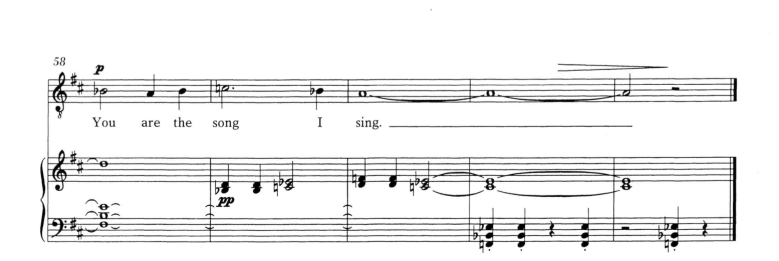

You are the song I sing. _____

4. Unspoken Thoughts at Bedtime

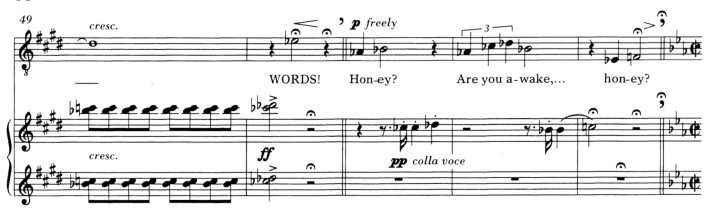

WORDS! Hon-ey? Are you a-wake,... hon-ey?

Peacefully ♩ = ca. 66

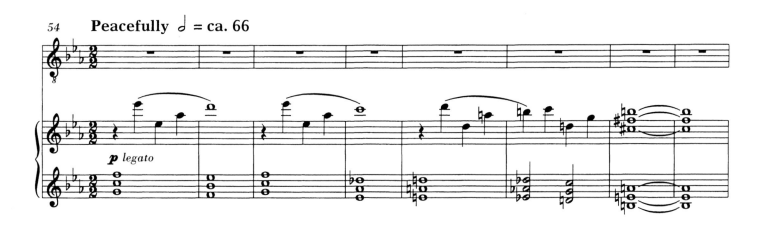

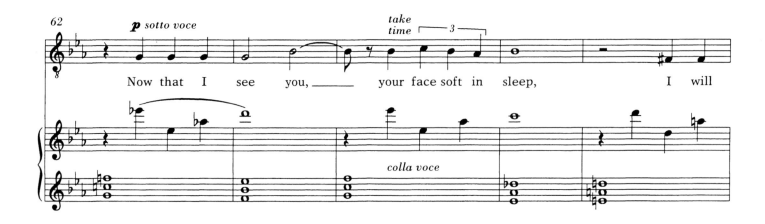

Now that I see you,_____ your face soft in sleep, I will

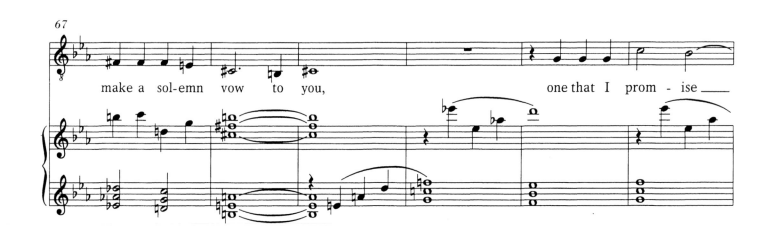

make a sol-emn vow to you, one that I prom - ise_____

What Lips My Lips Have Kissed

Edna St. Vincent Millay

Jake Heggie

* For separate cello part, see Appendix (p. 77).

kissed, and where and why _____ I have for-got-ten, and what arms have

lain un-der my head 'til morn - ing; ___ but the

rain is full of ghosts to-night, that

birds   have van-ished   one   by __ one, __   yet knows its   boughs more

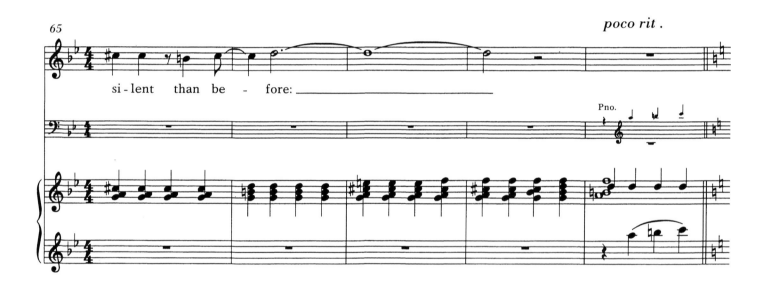

si - lent   than be - fore: _____

Tempo I

I can-not say __ what loves have come   and gone: I on - ly

know that ____ sum-mer sang in me ____ a lit-tle while,

that in me sings ____ no more.

My True Love Hath My Heart

Sir Philip Sydney

Jake Heggie

My _____ true love _____ hath my

heart   and I have his, _____   By just ex - change,   one   for   the

* For separate cello part, see Appendix (p. 78).
  If performing without cello, begin at measure 5.

* Play small notes when performing without cello.

My True Love Hath My Heart

Sir Philip Sydney

Jake Heggie

Moderately – not slow

Soprano

Mezzo-Soprano

Violoncello*

Piano

My ___ true love ___ hath my

heart and I have his, ___

By just ex - change,   one   for   the

* For separate cello part, see Appendix (p. 78).
  If performing without cello, begin at measure 5.

54

for Flicka
He's Gone Away

American folk song

arranged by Jake Heggie

Andante – very free – no sense of barlines

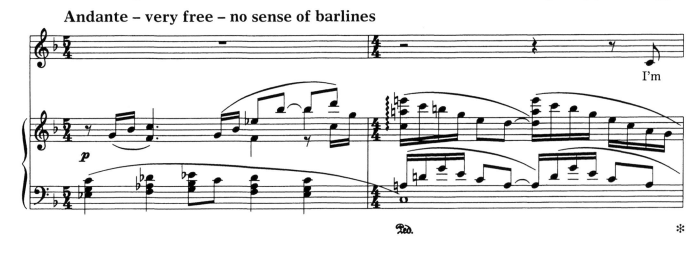

I'm

going a - way for to stay a lit-tle while But I'm

com-ing back if I go ten thou - sand miles. Oh

rit. *a tempo*

for Flicka

Barb'ry Allen

American folk song

arranged by Jake Heggie

'Twas in the mer - ry month of May when all the flowers were

bloom-ing, ___ Sweet Wil-liam on his ___ death-bed lay for love of Bar - b'ry

Al-len, ___ Sweet Wil-liam on his ___ death-bed lay for love of Bar - b'ry

Al - len.
As she was walk - ing through the field

she heard the death bells ___ knell-ing ___ and with ev - 'ry toll they___

seemed to say, "Hard - heart-ed Bar - b'ry Al - len." ___

"Oh, Moth-er, Moth - er, make my bed. And make it long and

nar-row; ___ Sweet Wil-liam died for _

me to-day, I'll die for him to - mor-row." _

poco rit.

pp *mysteriously*

They bur-ied Wil-liam in the old church-yard, And Bar-b'ra there a - nigh him. And out of his grave grew a red, red rose, and out of hers a bri-ar. They lapped and tied in a true love's knot. The rose ran 'round the bri-ar.

for Flicka

The Leather-Winged Bat

American folk song

arranged by Jake Heggie

"Hi," said the lit-tle ol'   leath-er-winged bat,

"I will tell you the rea - son that,   the rea - son   that   I   fly   in the night:

Hi - o day - o did-dle-o - down did-dle did-dle dum da day - o.

"Hi," said the blue - bird as he flew,

"Once I court - ed a young gal, too.

She got sass-y and want-ed to go,

legato

murmerando

hazy Ped.

Slower   Tempo I

So I tied a new string to my bow."   Hi - o day-o did-dle-o-down

colla voce

no Ped.

Hi - o day-o did-dle-o-day   Hi - o day-o did-dle-o-down   did-dle did-dle dum da-

day - o. _____

hazy Ped.

mp a piacere

"Hi," said the Rob-in as he flew,   "When I was a young man I'd court two. If

p colla voce

for Frederica von Stade, remembering Jo

Danny Boy

Frederick Weatherly

arranged by Jake Heggie

Oh, Dan - ny boy, the pipes, the pipes are call - ing _____ from glen to glen and down the moun - tain - side; _____ The sum - mer's gone, and all the ros - es fall - ing, _____

13
'Tis you, 'tis you must go, and I must bide. ___

17
But come ye back when

21
sum - mer's in the mea - dow ___ or when the val - - ley's

25
hushed and white with snow; 'Tis I'll be here in

dead, as dead I well may be, _____ You'll come and

find the place where I am ly - - ing, _____ And kneel and

say an "A - ve" there for me. _____

And I shall hear, though soft you tread a -

bove ___ me, _____ And e'en my grave will sweet - er, warm - er

be, For you will kneel and tell me that you

love ___ me, _____ And I shall sleep in peace un -

til you come to me. _____

Away in a Manger

melody by William James Kirkpatrick
arranged by Jake Heggie

VIOLONCELLO

Edna St. Vincent Millay

Appendix
What Lips My Lips Have Kissed

Jake Heggie

My True Love Hath My Heart

Sir Philip Sydney

Jake Heggie

Moderately – not slow